GORGIAS THEOLOGICAL LIBRARY

Volume 8

General Editor

George Anton Kiraz

The *Gorgias Theological Library* brings back to active circulation carefully selected rare classics which are essentials for the shelves of every theological library. These gems of scholarship remain primary sources of reference in modern research, yet they are inaccessible as not many libraries hold them. The selections include tools for the scholars, but also general theological works of interest to the general reader. Each of the volumes is carefully selected by the Gorgias editorial team based on its relevance to ongoing research and rarity.

Christianity and History

Christianity and History

ADOLF HARNACK

GORGIAS PRESS
2006

ISBN 1-59333-461-3

GORGIAS PRESS
46 Orris Ave., Piscataway, NJ 08854 USA
www.gorgiaspress.com

CONTENTS

INTRODUCTORY NOTE

———✦———

THE *following essay was originally pub-
lished in the form of a lecture ; and it was
delivered to the members of that branch of
the Evangelical Union which is established
in Berlin.*

*The Union is a remarkable feature of
the present state of religious life in modern
Germany. It was founded in* 1887 *after
the conclusion of the* Kulturkampf, *with the
professed object of protecting the interests
of Protestantism against the increasing
power of the Roman Church. In that
respect it bears some resemblance to certain*

7

associations and alliances in England; but its scope is much wider than theirs, its spirit is more liberal, and its work and influence have obtained a larger measure of success. The Union is fortunate, perhaps, in having no call to devote attention to ceremonial anomalies in the Churches to which its members belong; nor are its energies consumed in discussing the relative advantages of looking to the East or to the North at a particular juncture, or the appropriate shape and colour of ecclesiastical vestments.

Its time and strength are employed on the endeavour to preserve the Christian faith, as revealed in the Gospels, pure and undefiled. The members believe that where the Curia has wrought its will, it has disseminated superstition and exercised an intolerable tyranny; and although they represent a great variety of opinion, they are united in combating the influence of Rome, whether in the religious or in the political life of the Fatherland. To suppose that most of them are fanatics— and it is a common supposition in these days in regard to any body of militant Protestants — would be to do them a grievous injustice. They rest their belief on a calm review of the facts of history, and their resolution is the outcome, not of any sectarian prejudice, but of an intelligent desire to promote whatsoever things are wholesome and true.

While resistance to the doctrine and the policy of the Roman Church is the chief business of the Union, it has other objects which it seems to pursue with no less zeal.

Among them is the defence of Christianity in the face of the difficulties which it has had to encounter at the hands of philosophy and science.

Here as in Germany and elsewhere, those who adopt or profess this faith are guided by very diverse motives. There are many who endeavour to shape their lives in accordance with its precepts; there are others who embrace it out of sheer alarm; others, again, who affect both the creed and the practice of it; and not a few, like the magistrates in Gibbon's ironical analysis, who regard it as useful for political or social purposes. Finally, there is a large number of men and women who are outwardly adherents of the faith, but treat it with indifference or contempt.

Not alone among the members of the

German Evangelical Union, but in any large society of Christians anywhere, there are likely to be representatives of every one of these classes; and the attitude of them all is in some degree affected by any attack upon the Christianity which they profess in common. They meet the attack in various ways, according to the bent of their temper, the range of their knowledge, or the conceptions which they have formed or inherited. The Union embraces almost every known species of the Protestant theory of Christianity, between the extremes of unlimited indulgence in personal judgment and the narrowest bibliolatry. Within its circle the most unquestioning bigot may sit down with a rigorous historian or an uncompromising critic; and as in other controversies, the lines of defence largely depend for their strength and character upon the personality of the apologist.

When in October last the authorities of the branch of the Union in Berlin invited Professor Harnack to inaugurate a course of lectures, and that eminent scholar chose the relation between Christianity and history for his theme, the adherents of every grade of opinion found themselves in the company of a fellow-member who, by his own special studies and achievements, had earned the title not only of an exact historian, but also of an acute and far-seeing critic. As it was my privilege to be on a visit to Professor Harnack at the time, I had an opportunity of observing the profound attention with which his remarks were followed by a very large *audience, and of comparing or contrasting the reception which an address of this nature, delivered by a speaker of the like distinction, would have met with at home. It must be confessed that in this country, even outside the ranks of those who call themselves orthodox, the German historian, or the German critic, is sometimes regarded as a kind of literary Gorgon, who, if he fixes his gaze upon the field of theological inquiry, drives all the religion out of it and turns it to stone. The orthodox can hardly be brought to admit that, although he may have given long and serious attention to the problems involved in that study, he may yet be quite a respectable person, and as devout a Christian as any of themselves. It occurred to me that I might be of some service in helping to dispel this curious delusion, and at the same time assist in spreading a view of the relation between Christianity and history, as it was conceived by one of the most competent judges in Europe, if I translated this lecture, which was of a character to claim the interest of all thoughtful persons everywhere.*

Its object is to show in what sense religion, and more especially the Christian religion, can be said to be dependent upon historical facts: how far it is established, if certain alleged events are proved to have actually happened; how far it is overthrown, if they are found to be the product of myth or incredible legend. Among those who profess themselves adherents of this religion, and also among

*those who do not or cannot accept it,
there is a growing tendency to assume that
the result of historical criticism is to
shake its foundation; and this belief,
while it fills some persons with satisfaction
and others with dismay, leads a still
larger number to seek support for their
faith in a refusal to listen to any argu-
ment at all.*

*But the belief that the Christian religion
has been undermined by historical criticism
is largely due to ignorance, or at least to
a radical diversity of opinion, in regard
to the nature of its foundation. There
is a great difference, as Lessing argued,
between the Christian religion and Christ's
religion; between the structure of dogma
erected by Greek philosophy on a Jewish
soil, and the faith held by Christ himself,—*

the simple faith which every man can hold in common with him. Whatever may be obscure or doubtful in the narrative of the Gospels, the nature of Christ's faith and the purport of his teaching are clear and unmistakable ; and, in the main, they can be separated from alien accretions of later growth. It is Christ's own faith, rather than a series of subtle and complicated dogmas, which should form the foundation and the substance of the religion that is called by his name. This, I take it, is the view of Christianity that is adopted in the following pages.

T. BAILEY SAUNDERS.

February 1896.

CHRISTIANITY

AND

HISTORY

———◆———

*THE name of Jesus Christ of Nazareth
. . . neither is there salvation in any
other: for there is no other name under
heaven given among men, whereby we may
be saved.*

Such is the creed of the Christian Church.
With this creed she began; in the faith of
it her martyrs have died; and to-day, as
eighteen hundred years ago, it is from this
creed that she derives her strength. The
whole meaning and purport of religion,—
life in God, the forgiveness of sins, consola-

2

tion in suffering,—she couples with Christ's person; and in so doing she associates everything that gives life its significance and its permanent value, nay the Eternal itself, with an historical fact; maintaining the indissoluble, unity of both.

But is such a connexion defensible? Will it bear intelligent examination? When all history seems to be a ceaseless process of growth and decay, is it possible to pick out a single phenomenon and saddle it with the whole weight of eternity? especially when it is a phenomenon of the past.

If Christ's person were still among us, the matter would perhaps be different. But although we are separated from it by many centuries and an intricate and confusing tradition, we are told, nevertheless, that we must cling to it as though it were endowed with an eternal presence, and acknowledge it as the rock of our life. Is that possible? Is it right? This is a question which has occupied thoughtful Christians in all ages, and it involves the most careful inquiry into the essential nature and the just claims of Christianity; in a word, into the relation between Christianity and history. All that I can attempt in these brief pages is to indicate the nature of the question, and to offer some considerations by which its meaning and importance may be estimated.

I may begin by mentioning the encouraging fact that the great assault made by the eighteenth century on the connexion between religion and history has been repelled. This assault found its pregnant expression in the principle laid down by Lessing: *Historical truth, which is acci-*

dental in its character, can never become the proof of the truths of Reason, which are necessary.

The principle may, indeed, be right; everything depends upon the way in which it is construed. But in the way in which it was understood by Lessing's own generation, influenced as that generation was by Rousseau, it is wrong. It is the outcome of the whole of the superficial philosophy of the eighteenth century. According to that philosophy, everything that has happened in the way of history is of trivial moment; it is an accident; nay, it even cramps and fetters the mind; and there is no salvation anywhere but in the two forces which that generation described as *Nature* and *Reason*. They were regarded as forces that were invariable and constituted once for all; and no true blessing was to be obtained outside of them. It was believed that every man from the creation downwards possessed in his reason a fixed capital, which was capable of supplying him with everything that might be needful for a virtuous and happy life. It was believed, further, that man was fitted into the framework of nature, and was in harmony with it; and that he had only to unfold his powers in accordance with nature, in order to become a glorious specimen of his kind.

In this view of the world, history was no longer a necessity; for a man could receive absolutely nothing from it which he did not already possess. To the consistent adherents of this view, its logical outcome was that history seemed a strange and wrong-headed venture ; and the cry was all for renouncing its tyranny, and for returning to the freedom of nature. It is true that Lessing himself made great efforts to do justice to history ; but his efforts were uncertain, and they were but little understood. His generation had no concern for anything but the truths of reason, alleged to be eternal, and the "natural religion" which it had rediscovered ; and in possession of these blessings, it looked down on "the accidents of history" with contempt, and cut the bond between them and religion. All historical religions, so the eighteenth century taught, are at the best only the one true, natural religion in disguise, — the religion which always was and always will be,—and of this religion Reason, fixed and unalterable, is the only content. By the side of it, even Christianity and its founder can make no special or particular claim; for everything that is particular is accidental, superfluous, and intellectually mischievous.

Now to-day this view of the world is not, it is true, extinct; but it has been refuted. In no respect has the spirit of the nineteenth century so strongly opposed the spirit of the eighteenth, as in this.

It is a change which we owe to Herder and the leaders of the romantic movement; we owe it to Hegel and his great pupil Ranke; we owe it, not least of all, to the powerful reaction of the Christian faith. The illusion of a ready-made reason, existing from the beginning, has been dispelled; the idol of a "divine nature" has been unmasked; the vast problem involved in

the facile notion of a "natural religion"
has been revealed.   In the place of shallow
talk about divine nature and profane history, about the "eternal truths of reason"
and casual records, we have arrived at
the knowledge of *history*; of the history
from which we have received what we
possess, and to which we owe what we
are.   In this process two conceptions,
above all, came to the front with increasing clearness: *development* and *personality*.   They involve an opposition; but
it is an opposition which determines the
work of the historian in dealing with his
facts.

When the meaning of history came to
be accurately understood, religion was
restored to its place; for religion is no
ready-made structure, but a growth; and

it is a growth that falls within the history of humanity. Its developments are no mere outward semblance : they are a reality. Its prophets and founders have been prophets and founders indeed; for they have raised humanity to a higher level. Reverence for the spirit that prevails in history, and gratitude to all those from whom we have received any benefit, — and without it we should have been the poorer in our inner and outer life,—must, therefore, govern our views of that science.

Here we have a critical spirit very different from that which pervaded the so-called age of illumination. The assault which the eighteenth century directed against the connexion between history and religion has, in fact, proved a failure. But other assaults have been taking shape in

our own time. There is a whole array of
them.

The first proposition that meets us is
this : It is just because the Christian religion is a part of history, and consequently
of that *development* of which all history
consists, that it is no more than a link
in that development; and therefore its
founder cannot be allowed any peculiar or
unique position.

We succeed, let us say, in defeating this
attack. A fresh opponent then starts up
with the objection that even though the
founder of the Christian religion may have
been an incomparable man, he lived many
centuries ago; and it is therefore impossible
to go to him with our troubles and sorrows,
and to lay hold of him as the rock of our
life: it is not the *person* which we have

any longer to consider, but the *doctrine*, the *principle*.

If, in the end, this opponent be also routed, there is still one more. We are told that we may speak of Jesus Christ as we will, and he may have been all that we say, but that we cannot be certain of it; for where our idea of him has not been destroyed by historical criticism, it has been rendered doubtful; and, even though it were more trustworthy than it is, still the facts of history can never be known with a certainty that would entitle us to make them the foundation of our religious belief.

These are the three barriers that have been opposed to the creed of the Church on the score of history; and it is on these three questions that the whole of the controversy turns. Every form of doubt,

whether secret or open, deals in the main
with these questions; and in some shape
or other they are doubts which have been
entertained and pondered by us all.

I

PERSONALITY AND DEVELOPMENT

Now, as regards the first assault : it is the most comprehensive, but also the weakest, of the three.

It is perfectly true that the strength of our modern conception of history lies in the effort which we everywhere make to trace the *development* of things, and to show how one thing has grown out of another. That this is the true task of the historian is a proposition which can no longer be disputed. There can be no manner of doubt that it is only by this method that a true understanding of history can be attained; and even those who condemn the modern science of history cannot escape the influence of its method. They do the same work as is done by those whom they condemn, but they do not succeed in doing it so well; nay, they do it badly and imperfectly.

However, a man must be infatuated to maintain that, because all history is a history of development, it can and must be described as a process of material or mechanical change. Up till now the attempts that have been, and are still being, made in this direction carry their own refutation with them. At the very most, it is only in the sphere of political economy that we can trace a certain stringent order of phenomena, where the struggle for material existence is supreme; but even there this stringent order is always being disturbed by elements of a non - material character, which exert a powerful influence.

In the history of intellectual and moral ideas, the rough-and-ready way of explaining cause by environment alone breaks down altogether. I admit that even here much may be accounted for in this way, much more than earlier generations suspected : the necessity that drives and compels has often been the mother of progress; and even to-day we can see causes at work, and watch the process of growth. But without the strength and the activity of an individual, of a *personality*, nothing great, nothing that will bring us farther on our way, can be accomplished.

Whence comes the strength of the strong, and the deed of the doer? Whence comes it that the knowledge that might advance us, the thought that might save us, is transmitted from one generation to another as barren and worthless and dead as a stone, until some one seizes it and strikes it into fire? Whence comes that higher order of marriage, where a thought so unites with a soul that each is merged in the other, and belongs to the other, and masters the will? Whence comes the courage that conquers the resistance of a dull and unfeeling world? Whence comes the living power that begets a living conviction?

It is a very limited psychology which fails to see that these are the real levers of history. All that its adherents ask is whether the man has said anything new; and if so, whether it cannot be deduced from something that went before; and they profess themselves content if they ascertain that it was only "relatively" new, and that nothing very wonderful has happened after all. No! not only in the beginning was the Word, the Word that was at once Deed and Life; but the living, resolute, indomitable Word, namely, the *person*, has always been a power in history, along with and above the power of circumstance. Here, too, it is true, there are intervening links and developments. No torch lights itself; one prophet rouses another; but this mysterious development we can never fathom—we can only feel it.

What is true of history in general, and of all the lines on which intellectual and spiritual life is enacted, is true in the highest sense of religion, which is the profoundest subject of which history treats. *Man shall not live by bread alone, but by every word that proceedeth out of the mouth of God.* Never have the two great central elements of all life and action been more clearly and simply expressed; and our historians still have a lesson to learn from these words, if they are not to lose their way.

Of religion it is true that it, too, has been developed, and that it is in a state of constant development. From its history it may be shown that it has had to yield to the stress of trouble and danger: the trouble that teaches men to pray, the danger that deadens them and makes them grasp at a straw. But the same history tells us also, that no aspiration and no progress have ever existed without the miraculous exertion of an individual will, of a *person*. It was not what the person said that was new and strange,—he came when the time was fulfilled and spoke what the time required,—but how he said it; how it became in him the strength and power of a new life; how he transmitted it to his disciples. That was his secret, and that was what was new in him. Mankind looks up with reverence to all the great minds that have been given to it,—the thinkers, the artists, the heroes,—but it is only the prophets and the founders of religion that it worships; for it feels that here a power has been at work which frees it from the world, and lifts it above the things of every day.

But if we thus put all prophets and founders of religion into one class, it may be said that we, in our turn, are doing away with the significance of the founder of the Christian religion. That is certainly not the case; for there is no concrete or specific conception embracing the differences to be found among those whom we rightly call prophets and founders of religion. Every one of them is a power for himself, and must be judged by himself. There have been founders of religion both sacred and profane; there have been sublime prophets and strange prophets. An inexhaustible wealth of gift and power has been diffused among them; but the measure of it, their bearing, the goal of their efforts, every circumstance of their lives, differs with each of them. If this difference were disregarded, nothing would be clear. It would be a piece of presumptuous folly to attempt to lay down, at the outset, the measure of the Spirit—that is, of the Spirit of God—which has borne sway in these individuals.

But it is only of One that we know that he united the deepest humility and a purity of will with the claim that he was more than all the prophets who were before him: the Son of God. Of him alone we know that those who ate and drank with him, glorified him not only as their Teacher, Prophet, and King, but also as the Prince of Life, as the Redeemer and Judge of the world, as the living power of their existence—*it is not I that live, but Christ in me;*—and that presently a band of the Jew and Gentile, the wise and the foolish, acknowledged that they had received, from the abundance of this one man, grace for grace. This fact, which lies open to the light of day, is unique in history; and it requires that the actual personality behind it should be honoured as unique.

II

THIS disposes of the first objection : that no special or unique position can be attributed to the person of Jesus Christ, because of the presumption that all history takes the form of development.

But now we have to deal with a serious attack. Even though the founder of the Christian religion may have been an incomparable man, he lived, we are told, many centuries ago ; and therefore it is impossible to take him up into our religious life, and adopt him as its foundation : it is no longer the person that we have to consider, but the doctrine, or, as it is sometimes called, the *principle.* Nay, the objection is still more severely stated thus : Religion is wholly a matter of relation to God—God and the soul, the soul and God;— everything that intrudes upon this mutual relation destroys its exclusive character, and impairs its fervour and its freedom.

I might try to meet this attack by referring to the ecclesiastical doctrine of redemption and reconciliation through Jesus Christ; but I am afraid that if I did so I should hardly make myself clear; for in the form in which the Church has stated that doctrine, it belongs to the things which in these days are least understood, and therefore most open to doubt. Such is the fact; how far it is warranted is a matter of opinion. I shall therefore attempt to proceed by a different path.

Well then! it is quite true : religion is a relation of the soul to God, and nothing more. That a man should find God and possess Him as *his* God,—should live in the fear of Him, trust Him, and lead a holy and blessed life in the strength of this feeling,—that is the substance and the aim of religion. We can carry our conception of religion no further, nor can we allow any alien element to subsist alongside of it. Religion is ordering our ways and committing our troubles to the love and care of Him who rules—

" Befiehl Du Deine Wege und was Dein Herze kränkt,
Der allertreusten Pflege dess, der den Himmel lenkt." [1]

---

[1] Paul Gerhardt, the well-known German hymn-writer of the seventeenth century.— TR.

The stronger and purer our feeling of devotion, the more surely is it comprehended in this utterance. It is a truth which has been attested by Christ's disciples in all ages; it was attested by Christ himself in teaching us the Lord's Prayer; and therefore we cannot condemn the theologians who tell us that it is the sum and substance of religion.

But what holds good of all moral ideas, holds good in the highest sense of religion : it is one thing to be sensible of their truth, it is another to be possessed of their power. We may recognise and acknowledge the claims of the Christian religion, the peace and beauty of the religious life, and yet be quite incapable of raising ourselves to its level. It may hover before our eyes and shine with the radiance

of a star; and yet not burn like a fire in
our hearts. We may have the keenest
sense of the bonds that we would escape,
and yet be totally unable to set ourselves
free. Not only may we be so—we are so.
There is no one who has had this feeling,
or who has it again and again, and is
delivered from it, but knows that he has
been delivered because God has spoken to
him. The man who fails to hear the voice
of God for himself is without religion.
Speak, Lord, for Thy servant heareth, is
the only form in which a religious life is
possible.

As the conduct of human life is manifold and various, so, too, is the voice of
God. But we know that there are few
among us who hear and understand the
voice of God, in the secret sphere of their

inner personal life, without human help and
intervention.   The truth is, rather, that
one Christian educates another ; heart
kindles heart ; and the strength to will
what we approve comes from the mysterious Power by which one life awakens
another.   At the end of the series of
messengers and agents of God stands Jesus
Christ.   They point back to him, and it
is from him that has sprung the river of
life which they bear in themselves as their
own.   Various indeed is the measure of
their conscious relation to him—who could
deny it !—but they all live on him and
through him.

Here we have a fact which gives an incomparable significance to this personality,
as a force still working in history.   But
the objection with which we have to deal

is not yet exhausted. Jesus Christ, it is
said, remains, after all, a power of the
past; although it is a power which con-
tinues in effect. But when the Christian
faith sends us back to him, that is not
the view which it takes. We must endeavour to get a closer grasp of what this
faith means, in order to understand how
far its view is right, supposing that the
faith is right at all.

The Christian faith is not, as is so
often maintained, a gentle exaltation of
our earthly life, or a comfort and relief in
its troubles and trials. No! it is decision
for God and against the world. It is an
eternal life that is involved: the recog-
nition that in and above Nature and her
changes there is a realm of sanctity and
love, a city not built with hands, whose

citizens we are to be; and with this message there comes to us the demand that we should cleanse our hearts and deny ourselves.

We are here confronted with an alternative which determines our inner life. It is, indeed, a contest; but is victory possible? is there then, in truth, a higher Reality, compared with which the world is as nothing? or do our feelings and presentiments delude us? May it not be that we are altogether confined within the sphere of mechanical nature, the sphere of our earthly existence, and that we are waging a miserable war with our own shadows, with phantoms and spectres? That is the question of questions, the doubt of doubts.

Well! as long as the Christian faith has

existed, these doubts and questions have
been resolved by looking to Jesus Christ:
resolved, not in the form of philosophical
demonstration, but by looking with a con-
fident trust to the image of his life.
When God and everything that is sacred
threatens to disappear in darkness, or our
doom is pronounced; when the mighty
forces of inexorable nature seem to over-
whelm us, and the bounds of good and
evil to dissolve; when, weak and weary,
we despair of finding God at all in this
dismal world—it is then that the personality
of Christ may save us. Here we have a
life that was lived wholly in the fear of
God—resolute, unselfish, pure; here there
glows and flashes a grandeur, a love, which
draws us to itself. Although it was all a
continual struggle with the world; though

bit by bit one earthly possession after
another fell away, and at last the life
itself came to an ignominious end; yet no
soul can avoid the thought that whoso dies
thus, dies well : he dies not, but lives.
For it was in this life and death that there
first dawned upon mankind the assurance
of an eternal life, and a divine love which
overcomes all evil, nay, sin itself.   It is in
the presence of a glory which is beyond
the reach of death, that we have come to
perceive the vanity of the world and of all
earthly possessions.

Eighteen hundred years separate us from
this history; but if we seriously ask ourselves what it is that has given us the
courage to believe that in the history of
the world God prevails, not only by moral
and intellectual forces, but by His presence

in the midst of it; if we ask what it is
that leads us to believe in an eternal life—
our answer is, that we make bold to believe
it in reliance upon Christ. *Jesus lives, and
with him I live also.* He is the firstborn
among many brothers; he is our surety for
the reality of a future world.

So it is, then, that God speaks to us
through him. It was testified of Christ
that he was the *Way*, the *Truth*, and the
Life; as such he is still revealed to our
inmost feelings, and therein consists his
presence to us. As surely as everything
depends on the soul finding God and be-
coming one with Him, so surely is he the
true Saviour, Guide, and Lord who leads
the soul to God. When the Christian
Church proclaims of him that he lives,
it is a truth which is still attested to-day;

4

and the Church is also right in reminding
us of his sufferings and his death. But
we will not speak of these things now; nor
will we speak of them at all after the fashion
in which they are so often treated. That
the sufferings of the just form the saving
element in history, is a truth which we
feel in the measure in which our senses are
alive to the gravity of the moral issue, and
open to the influence of personal sacrifice.
But "we draw a veil over the sufferings of
Christ, for the very reason that we hold
them in such reverence. In our judgment it is an unwarrantable and audacious
thing to treat these deep mysteries, in
which the divine depths of suffering lie
hidden, as an object of barter—to keep an
account in them, or to toy and trifle with
them; nor to rest until the most worthy

of all actions is made to look common
and insipid." [1]

We ought not to forget that faith in
Christ is never more than a mere cry of
Lord, Lord, if it does not pass into the
strength of allegiance in the good cause.
Not those did he himself call his brothers
and his sisters, who desired to see him,
or to raise aloft his name in the world;
but those who do the will of his Father
in heaven. It is by this utterance that
we have always to judge the Christian's
faith.

[1] Goethe.—TR.

III

THAT in spite of the eighteen hundred years
which separate us from him, Jesus Christ
can have, nay has, a place in the religious
life of the Christian ; that his personality,
and not his doctrine alone, is still to-day
set for the rising again of many—I have
tried to show.   But a third and final attack
confronts us.   You may, we are told, talk
of Jesus Christ as you will, and he may
have been all that you say, but you cannot
be certain of it ; for where our idea of
him has not been destroyed by historical

criticism, it has been rendered doubtful ; and even though it were more trustworthy than it is, still the facts of history can never be known with a certainty that would entitle us to make them the foundation of our religious belief.

This objection is the most serious of the three ; and if it were in all respects justifiable, it would go ill with us.

" Where our idea of him has not been destroyed by historical criticism, it has been rendered doubtful." At the first blush it looks as if this were indeed the case. I pass over such results of criticism as flourish to-day, and to-morrow are cast into the oven ; I speak only of those which are brought before us again and again with increasing force. If we direct our attention first of all to the external historical facts, we find that

the tradition as to the incidents attending
the birth and the early life of Jesus Christ
has been shattered; and so too has been the
credibility of many of the stories which were
told of him. We find, too, that criticism
cannot lay the ancient doubts raised by
the reports of what took place on the first
Easter morning. As regards the picture of
his life, as regards his discourses and the
doctrine he taught, the historical way of
looking at them seems to transform them
altogether.

The man who reads his Bible in a homely
way is wont to treat all the characteristic
features which he encounters in that book
as above and beyond time. He sees and
feels such things only as he takes to form
the true kernel of the narrative: things
which concern himself; and it was by

these that the Christian doctrine was
formerly established by the Church. But
the historical way of looking at them may
not, and will not, overlook the concrete
elements in and by which the life and the
doctrine were actually fashioned in their
day. It seeks for points of connexion with
the Old Testament and its developments,
with the religious life of the Synagogue,
with contemporary hopes for the future,
with the whole intellectual and spiritual
condition of the world of Greece and Rome;
and it finds that the evidence of such connexion is unmistakable. The consequence
is, that the sayings and discourses of the
Lord, and the image of his life itself, not
only take their colour—and it is a very
definite colour—from the history of the
time, but they are also seen to possess

certain definite limitations. They belong to their time and their environment; and they could not exist in any other. But they lose no particle of their power and validity, unless it can be shown that the main lineaments of the personality of Christ, and the sense and true point of his sayings, have been altered. I cannot discover that historical criticism has effected any such change.

The same is true of the testimony which he gave of himself. I admit that if historical research had proved that he was an apocalyptic enthusiast or a visionary, whose image and utterances were invested with a purity of aim and a sublimity of thought only by the refining influence of later times, it would be another matter. But who has proved that, and who could prove it? For

besides the four written Gospels we possess
a fifth, unwritten ; and in many respects
its voice is clearer and more effective than
those of the other four—I mean the united
testimony of the first Christian community.
It enables us to gather what was the pre-
vailing impression made by this personality,
and in what sense his disciples understood
his words and the testimony which he
gave of himself. It is true that his
clothes—the outward form of his doctrine
—were part of the heritage ; but the great
and simple truths which he came to preach,
the personal sacrifices which he made, and
his victory in death, were what formed the
new life of his community ; and when the
apostle Paul with divine power described
this life as a life in the Spirit,[1] and again

[1] Rom. viii.

as a life in love,[1] he was only giving back
the light which had dawned upon him in
and through Jesus Christ his Lord. This
is a simple matter of fact, which no historical criticism can in any way alter. All
that it can do is to place it in a clearer
light, and so increase our reverence for
the divinity which was revealed in radiance
in a Son of Abraham, amid the wreck and
refuse of a narrow world. Let the plain
Bible-reader continue to read his Gospels
as he has hitherto read them; for in the
end the critic cannot read them otherwise.
What the one regards as their true gist and
meaning, the other must also acknowledge
to be so.

But the facts, the facts! I do not know
how there can be a greater fact than the

[1] 1 Cor. xiii.

one which I have just been describing.
By the side of it, what can any historical
detail signify ?

We are told, however, that an historical
detail has a very obvious significance ;
that it is only the external fact, nay, the
miraculous fact, which can afford us the
final and only certainty that there exists
a reality corresponding to our belief ; that
the objects of our belief are not mere
phantoms of thought, but that God Himself governs the course of history, and is
leading it to its goal.

I am well aware of the gravity of
this assertion, and I am far from dis-
puting anyone's right to make it if he
chooses. If God would but rend the
heavens and come down, that we might
behold Him !—it is a cry that is often

heard. But I know, too, that it is not born out of the depth and strength of the faith which the apostle Paul describes, and that it readily falls under the utterance of the Lord: *Except ye see signs and wonders, ye will not believe.* Great is the power of external authority in. matters of religion; great is the power of signs and wonders; but only where their substance lies can faith and devotion find their ultimate assurance. Their substance is God the Lord; it is reliance on Jesus Christ, whose word and spirit are even to-day a witness to the heart of the power of God.

Woe to us if it were otherwise; if our faith rested on a number of details, to be demonstrated and established by the historian. It would be mere sophistry for any historian to claim that he had achieved such a task; for it is assuredly true that no detail of the past can attain such a degree of evidential certainty that it could form the foundation for bricks and mortar, let alone a whole eternity. Testimonies, documents, assertions—when all is said, to what do they amount?

There is, I admit, a difference between fact and fact. The actual external details are always a matter of controversy; and in this sense Lessing was perfectly right when he warned us against coupling matters of the highest moment with " accidental truths of history," and hanging the whole weight of eternity on a spider's thread. But the spiritual purport of a whole life, of a personality, is also an historical fact: we are certain of it by the effect which it produces; and it is here that we find the link that binds us to Jesus Christ. It is a feeling which is one with devotion itself; and this is what the same Lessing meant when he spoke the word of deliverance: "Even though we may be unable to remove all the objections that may be made against the *Bible*, nevertheless, in the heart of all Christians who have attained to an inner sense of its essential truths, *Religion* remains steadfast and intact."

But are we to say that such external details as have been handed down are of no significance whatever? Who would be so shortsighted, or so frivolous, as to maintain such a proposition? Because we cannot build upon them, they are far from having no significance. First of

all, we have to examine whether they are
not actually true after all. Much that
was formerly rejected has been re-estab-
lished on a close investigation, and in the
light of comprehensive experience. Who
in these days, for example, could make
such short work of the miraculous cures
in the Gospels as was the custom of
scholars formerly?

Then, too, it may be said of all that is
told of Jesus Christ, that it is written as
a *lesson* for us. That is a consideration
which in our controversies is often unduly
overlooked; but it is in keeping with the
objects of the oldest writers, and the
practice of the oldest teachers. In matters
of religious tradition it is the peculiarity
of much that passes for historical, that
the spiritual meaning to be found in it

is its most important feature. Where something is maintained as an historical fact, it is more often than not a defence of the article of faith bound up with it. It is through the formula, *Conceived of the Holy Ghost*, that the dogma of the Divine Sonship of Jesus Christ is proclaimed; in and with the message of the Ascension we are taught that he lives and rules with the Father.

This leads us to another aspect of the religious significance of external details, which is closely related to that which I have been mentioning. They have been to faith what the prop is to the vine, or a sheltering screen to the tender plant. They have given it support and guidance, or they have protected its growth from the influence of wind and weather; and the

service which they have rendered in the
past, they still render to-day to many.
The difficulty is that one man's faith
requires a strong stake to prop it, or
some kind of protective shelter; whilst
another finds the prop break in his hands,
and his faith bloom only in the free light
of the sun.

Finally, much in the New Testament
that is recorded as history, much that
affects us most deeply, is not only told
us as a lesson, but, in the form in which
it is given, it possesses a deep *symbolical*
significance. I know none of the leading
events of the narrative of which that
cannot be said. The same spirit which
revealed to our eyes the power and the
glory of a divine life, so far as mankind
is able to grasp it, has also veiled the

5

truth for us with a delicate web of significant legend, a poetry that moves the heart, and has thus brought it home in picture and parable.

That the stories which are told of Christ possess this manifold significance, will be obvious to everyone who considers the history of Christianity with an open mind and a humble heart. It is an interpretation of the facts which is not without its dangers; for on the one hand it may readily lead a man to foist his own mind upon history, to confuse the plant with the prop, and so to conjure up grave difficulties; and on the other, it may deaden the force of historical facts as real facts, and the personality of Christ as a real personality. However, the difficulties which have arisen here are

not of our making, and we cannot
resolve them in any arbitrary fashion of
our own. Rather let us trust to that
divine guidance which knows what is
good for us; let us proclaim truly, and
with a pure mind, the knowledge which
we have received; and then let us
endeavour to understand the profound
saying, that natural strength and the
crutch that supports it come from the
same source—*Kräfte und Krücken kom-
men aus* EINER *Hand.*[1]

It may, perhaps, have been expected
that I should speak of other matters: of
the changes which Christianity has ex-
perienced in the course of its history, or of
the blessings which it has spread abroad
in the world. But a knowledge of the

[1] Goethe —TR.

fundamental question, namely, how far religion and history are connected, and how they are united in the evangelical faith, is more important than anything else. This evangelical faith need fear no test that can be applied to it. It can bear a strict and methodical scrutiny of the facts which form its historical foundation ; nay, for its own sake it must demand such a scrutiny ; for while it has no concern with Pilate's speculative question— what is truth ?—yet the knowledge of the truth is assigned as its mission, and there, too, its promise will be fulfilled.